HOLIDAY INN   MUSIC AND LYRICS BY IRVING BERLIN

Cover art by SpotCo

ISBN 978-1-4950-7400-4

Irving Berlin Music Company®
www.irvingberlin.com

EXCLUSIVELY DISTRIBUTED BY

7777 W. BLUEMOUND RD. P.O. BOX 13819 MILWAUKEE, WI 53213

Visit Hal Leonard Online at
www.halleonard.com

ROUNDABOUT THEATRE COMPANY | **50 YRS**

Todd Haimes, Artistic Director
Harold Wolpert, Managing Director
Julia C. Levy, Executive Director
Sydney Beers, General Manager
in association with
Universal Stage Productions
presents

HOLIDAY INN,
THE NEW IRVING BERLIN MUSICAL

Music and Lyrics by
Irving Berlin

Book by
Gordon Greenberg and Chad Hodge

Bryce Pinkham

Lora Lee Gayer   **Megan Lawrence**   **Megan Sikora**

with
Corbin Bleu
and
Lee Wilkof

with

Malik Akil   Will Burton   Barry Busby   Darien Crago   Caley Crawford   Jenifer Foote
Morgan Gao   Matt Meigs   Shina Ann Morris   Drew Redington   Catherine Ricafort
Amanda Rose   Jonalyn Saxer   Parker Slaybaugh   Samantha Sturm   Amy Van Norstrand
Travis Ward-Osborne   Paige Williams   Victor Wisehart   Kevin Worley   Borris York

Set Design **Anna Louizos**	Costume Design **Alejo Vietti**	Lighting Design **Jeff Croiter**	Sound Design **Keith Caggiano**
Orchestrations **Larry Blank**	Vocal and Dance Arrangements **Sam Davis**	Additional Dance and Vocal Arrangements **Bruce Pomahac**	Music Coordinator **John Miller**
Hair & Wig Design **Charles G. LaPointe**	Make-up Design **Joe Dulude II**	Associate Director **Andy Señor, Jr.**	Associate Choreographer **Barry Busby**
Production Management **Aurora Productions**	Production Stage Manager **Michael J. Passaro**	Casting **Jim Carnahan**, C.S.A. **Carrie Gardner**, C.S.A. **Stephen Kopel**, C.S.A.	Press Representative **Polk & Co.**
Associate Managing Director **Steve Dow**	Director of Marketing & Audience Development **Robert Sweibel**	Director of Development **Lynne Gugenheim Gregory**	
Founding Director **Gene Feist**	Adams Associate Artistic Director* **Scott Ellis**		

Executive Producer
Sydney Beers

Music Supervision and Direction by
Andy Einhorn

Choreography by
Denis Jones

Directed by
Gordon Greenberg

Major support for *Holiday Inn* is provided by The Blanche and Irving Laurie Foundation.
Holiday Inn benefits from Roundabout's Musical Theatre Fund with lead gifts from The Howard Gilman Foundation and Perry and Marty Granoff.

Originally produced by Goodspeed Musicals, Michael P. Price, Executive Producer

*Generously underwritten by Margot Adams, in memory of Mason Adams.

Roundabout Theatre Company is a member of the League of Resident Theatres.   www.roundabouttheatre.org

4   Steppin' Out with My Baby

8   Blue Skies

13 It's a Lovely Day Today

16 Plenty to Be Thankful For

20 Nothing More to Say

25 Shaking the Blues Away

30 White Christmas

34 Holiday Inn

37 Happy Holiday

40 Let's Start the New Year Right

43 You're Easy to Dance With

47 Be Careful, It's My Heart

51 Cheek to Cheek

56 Easter Parade

60 Song of Freedom

STEPPIN' OUT WITH MY BABY

Words and Music by
IRVING BERLIN

BLUE SKIES

Words and Music by
IRVING BERLIN

11

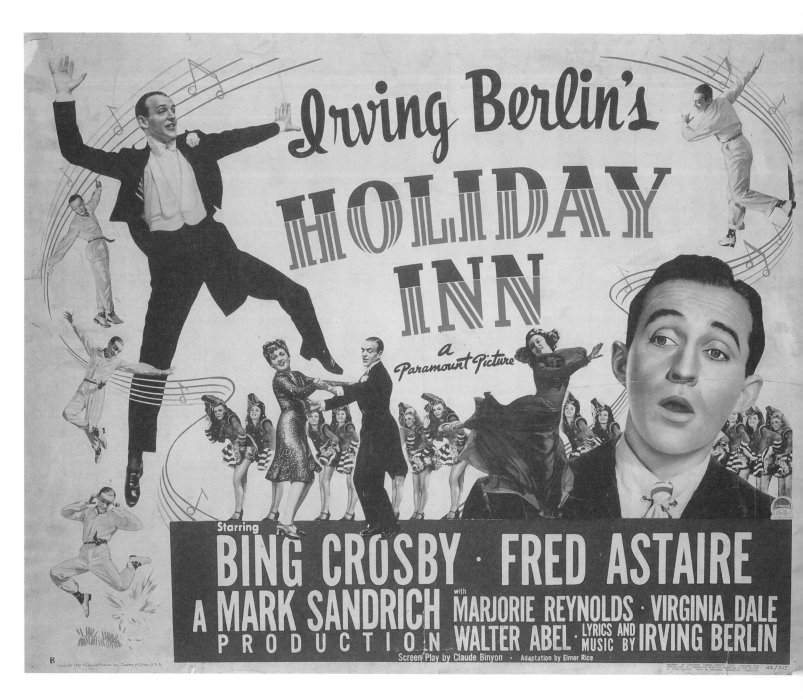

IT'S A LOVELY DAY TODAY

Words and Music by
IRVING BERLIN

PLENTY TO BE THANKFUL FOR

Words and Music by
IRVING BERLIN

Moderate Bounce tempo

I've got plen - ty to be thank - ful for. ___

I have - n't got ___ a great big yacht ___ to

sail from shore ___ to shore. ___ Still I've got plen -

NOTHING MORE TO SAY

Words and Music by
IRVING BERLIN

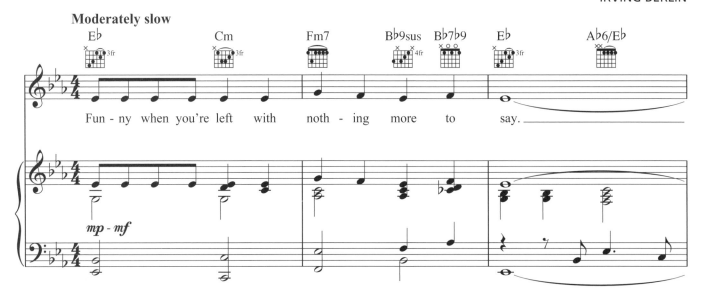

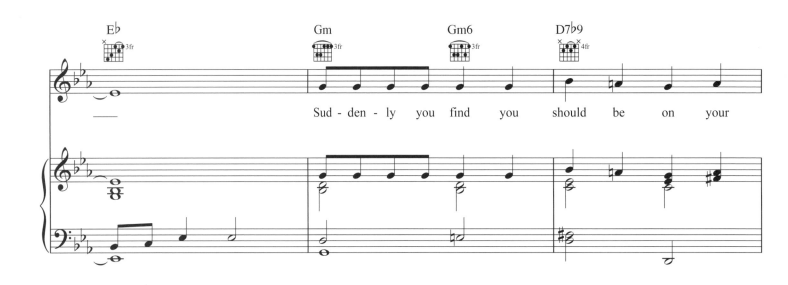

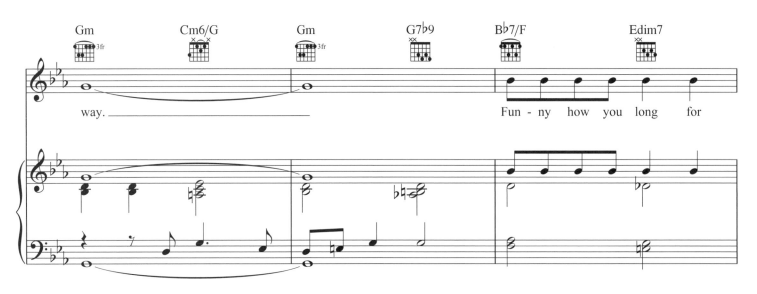

long - er come your way. _____

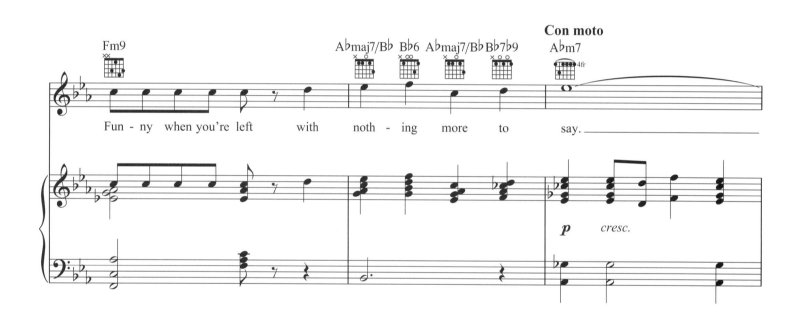

Fun - ny when you're left with noth - ing more to say. _____

SHAKING THE BLUES AWAY

Words and Music by
IRVING BERLIN

There's an old su-per-sti-tion

WHITE CHRISTMAS

Words and Music by
IRVING BERLIN

HOLIDAY INN

Words and Music by
IRVING BERLIN

HAPPY HOLIDAY

Words and Music by
IRVING BERLIN

Slowly

Hap - py hol - i - day, _____ hap - py hol - i - day. _____ While the mer - ry bells keep ring - ing, may your ev - 'ry wish come true. Hap - py

LET'S START THE NEW YEAR RIGHT

Words and Music by
IRVING BERLIN

YOU'RE EASY TO DANCE WITH

Words and Music by
IRVING BERLIN

BE CAREFUL, IT'S MY HEART

Words and Music by
IRVING BERLIN

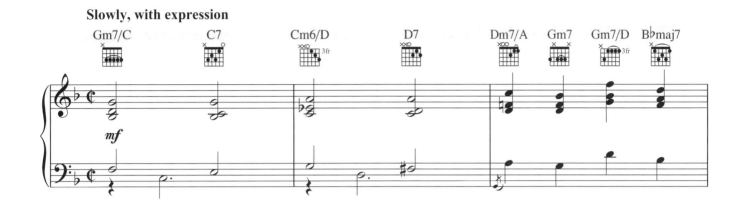

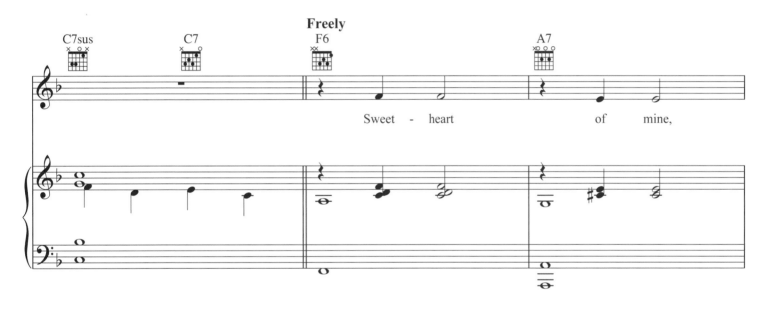

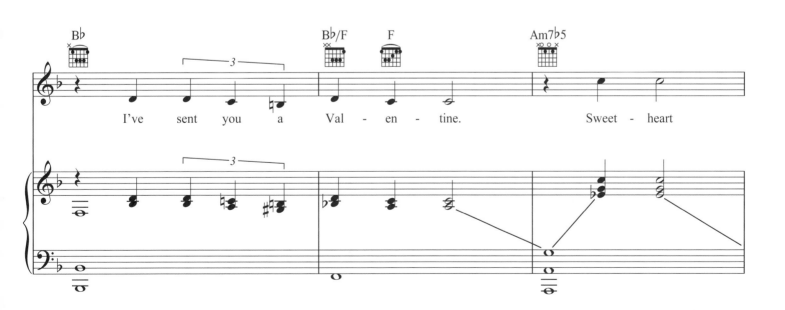

CHEEK TO CHEEK

Words and Music by
IRVING BERLIN

EASTER PARADE

Words and Music by
IRVING BERLIN

Nev - er saw you look quite so pret - ty be - fore. _____

_____ Nev - er saw you dressed quite so love - ly, what's more _____

SONG OF FREEDOM

Words and Music by
IRVING BERLIN